Gabriel Griffin

broken threads

for Kevin Bailey
with thanks
for his generous encouragement

Gabriel Griffin

broken threads

haiku~tanka~cherita

OPENING / SHUTTING

broken thread
no way now
out of the labyrinth

still wondering

which door

you opened when you left

leaving you forgot
to take the warmth
from our handshake

after the child goes
a silver balloon
playing on the ceiling

the church bell
behind
time

stopping
the heart waking
to life

LAKE

still
the lake
between two winds

a gladness of mayflies
rejoicing at dawn
swifts swoop

diving
into its shadow
black goose

lights on far banks
church blazing in hills
night fog has lifted

disappear appear
steps going down to the lake
appear disappear

fog over lake
the world has drifted
away from the island

GARDENS

blackbird's eggs
broken on the lawn
a silent spring

dusk
cold shadows fingering
hot flowers

frozen dawn
surviving the night
a robin clicks

butterfly kisses
frozen now in formalin.
spirits fluttering

FIELDS

rolling
across the fields
waves of lavender

in a lavender ocean
lockers of flowers
clammed with bees

in stubbled fields
bronze wheels
ready to roll in winter

hunter
in autumn fields
shooting spring song

stacks of prefabs
in a winter field
waiting for an earthquake

slabs of eternit
abandoned in a meadow
birthing litchen

MOUNTAINS

shadows lengthen
the mountain reclaims
its dowry of snows

in the mountain hut
ogre boots clumping
dwarves flee down slopes

stiff pine
all its christmasses
frozen to its boughs

pines snow-white
sleep in winter woods
gowned entombed in ice.

on the pinewood wall
of the winter cabin
a mountain goat stopped jumping

three crows at dusk
flying north
into an haiku

TRACKS

empty plastic bag
blowing down the track
getting there first

on volcanic shores

boatloads erupt

population explosion

CITY

cranes
calling on the city
to rise

so few umbrellas
passing in the street
give way to another

the two of us
under one umbrella
your husband looking

rain falling
forgetting
to open my umbrella

city umbrellas
lovers kiss the rain away
under black silk skies

unsure you're crying
or if it's raining
opening my umbrella

I YOU THEY

drought
swimming pool
overflowing

lighting the wood fire
a gold ring glinting
in last year's ashes

remembering the time
but not having the time
to remember the dream

summer evening
taking us all for a ride
merry-go-round

evening
only shadows
coming home

midnight bells sleep
frozen silence of stars
a stable sparkling

birds singing at dawn
you cannot hear them
yet turn in your sleep

stroking tabby hairs
on the old sweater
not worn since he died

always the wrong person
standing under the mistletoe
pressing the wrong kiss

your mistletoe kiss
bloodless as the berries
slippery as a druid's blade

christmas wreath
with plastic leaves for wishes
not biodegradable

inuits have no
word for lightning, We
have no word for

SEA

algae
weathered
memories

brine
pickled
summers

sea fog
our shouts
drown

winter beach
plastic bags
waving

wrack
vane
hopes

fishbone
gutted
passion

conch
forgotten waves
break in my head

when sea withdraws
whatever god you pray to
tsunamis come

CHERITA

we have their cold

deep in our bones
their hunger

in the pit of our stomachs
their gods
in the caves of our minds.

home-knitted mittens

ice sequinned
on the windowsill

kittens basking in the sun
soft fur hiding
sharpening nails.

holly pricks

ivy's a creep
pine's hands are sticky

wishing for mistletoe's
cloying pearls
its poisonous kiss

once

as many voices in this village
as cobbles

by day
we walk over them
at night they whisper over our beds

sudden cold

like whale
the mountain

swallows the sun.
an ocean of shadows
washes over land

thick clouds

conceal
mountains' radiance

i walk on
rain soaks
but does not stop me.

TANKA

september tides
cancel summer names

i spell your name in seashells

a hansel track back
to fairytales

roses violets lilies
flower-patterned

hand-me-downs

gardens she could never
quite get into

on each wind-chime
i hang a letter.

each time the door opens

the wind-bells
call your name.

Some of these poems have been published
in
Haiku Quarterly Poetry Magazine
edited by Kevin Bailey

Still, edited by Ai Li

The acorn book of contemporary haiku
edited by Lucien Stryk and Kevin Bailey
(UK 2000)

Cover photo by dids for pexels